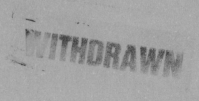

SOUND *and* VIBRATIONS

MAKING SENSE *of* SCIENCE

Peter Riley

FRANKLIN WATTS
LONDON•SYDNEY

First published in 2005 by Franklin Watts
96 Leonard Street, London EC2A 4XD

Franklin Watts Australia
45-51 Huntley Street, Alexandria, NSW 2015

Text copyright © Peter Riley 2005
Design and concept © Franklin Watts 2005

Series Editor: Rachel Cooke
Editor: Kate Newport
Art director: Jonathan Hair
Designer: Mo Choy
Illustrator: Ian Thompson

Picture credits:
Aero Graphics Inc/Corbis: 19b.
Ancient Art & Architecture Collection: 5b, 15tr.
Art Underground/Corbis: front cover main, 1, 20.
Tom Brakefield/Corbis: 25cl.. Corbis: 26c.
Greenpeace/Corbis Sygma: 28t.
Darrell Gulin/Corbis: 23tr.
Rune Hellestad/Corbis: 21b.
Dr Najeeb Layyous/Science Photo Library: 25br.
Michael Maconachie/Ecoscene: 22b, 23cl.
Joe McDonald/Corbis: 24.
Richard Megna/Fundamental/Science Photo Library: 17c.
Picturepoint/Topham: 15c, 29b. Popperfoto: 5c.
Chris Priest/Science Photo Library: 9b.
Alan Schein Photography/Corbis: 16t.
Science Museum, London/Topham: 10t.
Sciencephotos/Alamy: front cover inset, 13t.
Charles Walker/Topham: 17b.

Picture research: Diana Morris

All other photography by Ray Moller.

Every attempt has been made to clear copyright.
Should there be any inadvertent omission,
please apply to the publisher for rectification.

A CIP catalogue record for this book
is available from the British Library.

ISBN 0 7496 5530 5

Printed in Malaysia.

CONTENTS

FINDING OUT ABOUT SOUND

Hold this book up in front of your mouth, and say 'Ahhh…' for as long as you can. As you do this, move the book down away from your mouth and back up again a few times. The sound you are making will change. When the book is in front of your mouth, the sound is louder because it is reflected back to your ears. When the book is not in front of your mouth, the sound reflects from objects further away and is softer and quieter.

Scientists did not begin to investigate sound thoroughly until the 17th century. Since then, we have learned a lot more about the vibrations that we call sound – including the discovery of sounds we cannot hear (see pages 24–25).

SOURCES OF SOUND

Sound can be made in a variety of ways. Probably one of the earliest ways you learned to make sound was to shake a rattle. Inside a rattle, pieces of plastic bang against the sides to make the sound. Later you probably discovered that if you stretch an elastic band and pluck it, this makes a sound too. Another way to make a sound is to blow gently over the mouth of an empty bottle.

VOLUME OF SOUND

When they play your favourite song on the radio, you may turn the volume up to make it louder. Then someone else in the house might shout at you to turn the volume down! Sounds can vary in strength. A loud sound has greater strength than a quiet one.

HOW DOES THE VOLUME AFFECT HEARING?

Sit in a circle with several friends. Start a message going round the circle by speaking quietly to the friend on your left. When you get the message back from the friend on your right, is it the same as the one you sent? Now pass another message, but speak in a low whisper. Do you get the message back correctly this time?

HIGH AND LOW SOUNDS

Have you ever run your fingernail down a blackboard? It makes a horrible high screeching noise. In contrast, when the ball just misses the goal at a football match, the crowd makes a low groaning sound. These two sounds differ in something called pitch. The fingernail on the blackboard is a high-pitched sound, while the crowd's groan is a low-pitched one. Sounds can have a wide range of pitches.

Crowds at a match make a variety of low-pitched and high-pitched sounds.

ANCIENT SOUNDS

A study of ancient musical instruments shows that people in the distant past knew about how sounds were made. They knew for instance that if strings of different lengths or metal bells of different sizes were made to vibrate, they would make different sounds. By controlling these vibrations they could make a range of sounds that was pleasing to the ear – we call it music.

Aristotle (384–322 BC), a Greek scientist, believed that sounds travelled through the air in a similar way to waves travelling across a pond. He was close to the truth about this, but he also believed that high-pitched sounds travelled faster than low-pitched ones. If this were true, you would hear the high-pitched sound of a flute in a band sooner than the low thud of the bass drum. Of course this is not what happens: you hear the flute and drum sounds at the same time.

A bust of Aristotle. Another of his ideas was that echoes are sounds that bounce back to the ear 'like a ball thrown at the walls of this space.'

5

VIBRATIONS AND WAVES

The plucking of an elastic band gives a huge clue to how sounds are made. When an elastic band is plucked, it moves quickly to and fro. This is called vibrating. While the elastic band is vibrating, it produces a sound. When it stops vibrating, the sound stops too. Sounds are caused by vibrations.

A CLOSER LOOK AT VIBRATION

An elastic band is surrounded by air. Air is composed of miniscule particles called atoms and molecules. They are free to move about. When the elastic band vibrates, it moves one way and then the other way very quickly over and over again.

As the elastic moves to and fro, it pushes on the particles in the air close by. First it squashes them together, then it moves away and they can spread out again. So the vibration of the elastic band makes the nearby air particles vibrate, too.

These vibrations get passed on to air particles further and further away from the elastic band. The vibrations pass through the air as waves of high and low pressure – sound waves.

A vibrating elastic band causes waves of high and low pressure to spread out through the air around it. These are sound waves.

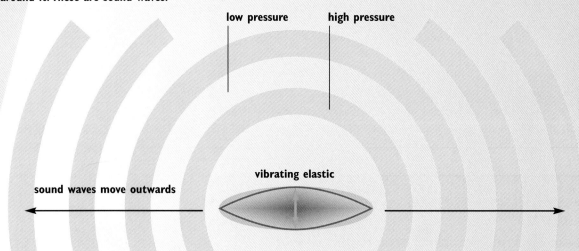

low pressure   high pressure

vibrating elastic

sound waves move outwards

TRANSFERRING VIBRATION

Attach a light ball, such as one used for table tennis, to one end of a thread with a piece of sticky tape. Hold up the ball on the thread and strike a tuning fork on a piece of wood. Hold the vibrating fork next to the ball and see the ball vibrate. It is behaving like an air particle.

Now strike the tuning fork again and dip the end in a bowl of water. You should see waves, and you may even get splashed.

Sound waves can travel through solids, liquids and gases, but they cannot travel through nothing at all (a vacuum). Otto Von Guericke (1602–1686), a German scientist, invented an air pump that could suck all the air out of a jar to create a vacuum. Robert Boyle (1627–1691), a British scientist, then made a similar jar and placed a bell in it and made it ring. He found that no sound was heard. Boyle had proved that sound could not travel through a vacuum. In space there is a vacuum, so sound cannot travel through space. When a spaceship explodes in a film it makes a great noise, but in reality there would not be a sound.

THE **HYDROPHONE**

The hydrophone is an underwater microphone (see pages 28–29) sealed in a special way so that water cannot reach its electrical parts. Hydrophones are used as part of a ship's sonar equipment and to record the sounds made by whales (see pages 24–25).

COMPARING SOUND IN AIR, WATER AND WOOD

Put an inflated balloon next to a loudly ticking clock. Press your ear gently against the balloon on the side away from the clock, and listen.

Now repeat the experiment using a balloon filled with water. When is the ticking louder?

Finally, put one end of a piece of wood on the clock and put your ear on the other end. How does the sound compare this time?

THE EAR

Have you noticed how people put a hand to their ear when they are trying to listen carefully to something? This tells us what the external part of the ear, the part we can see, does. It collects sounds. When someone cups their hand to their ear they are making the sound-collecting surface larger so that more sound passes into the ear.

Once sound waves enter the ear, things become much more complicated. The ear can be divided into three parts – the outer ear, the middle ear and the inner ear.

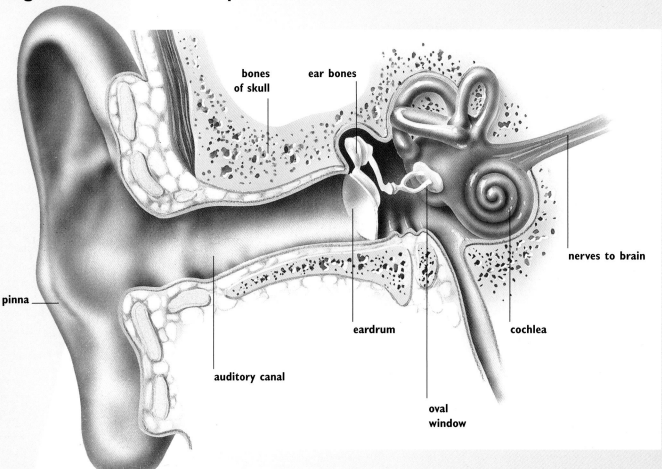

bones of skull

ear bones

nerves to brain

pinna

eardrum

cochlea

auditory canal

oval window

THE OUTER EAR

The external part of the ear is called the pinna. Sound waves reaching it are reflected into the ear and down a tube called the auditory canal. At the end of the tube is a membrane called the eardrum. The sound waves make the eardrum vibrate.

THE MIDDLE EAR

There are three tiny bones on the other side of the eardrum. They transmit the vibrations to another membrane called the oval window and make it vibrate too. The bones amplify the movements of the eardrum, so the vibrations of the oval window are stronger than those of the eardrum.

THE INNER EAR

The vibrations pass into a liquid behind the oval window and move through a coiled tube called the cochlea. In here are tiny hairs. The vibrations make the hairs move, and as they do so they cause nerves close by to fire off messages to the brain. As a result, we have the sensation of hearing the sound.

8

MAKING A DRUM VIBRATE

When sound vibrations reach the eardrum, they make it vibrate. You can see how this works by making a drum vibrate without touching it.

Put some sugar on a drum skin. This will help you see the vibration. Now hold a metal tray over the drum and hit the tray with a spoon. Sound waves from the tray strike the drum skin and make it vibrate. As the drum skin vibrates, the sugar grains bounce up and down.

THE EFFECT OF A HOLE IN THE EARDRUM

A common type of ear damage is a perforated eardrum (a hole in the eardrum). This experiment shows what effect a perforated eardrum has on hearing.

Hold a piece of soft tissue paper (the eardrum) lightly in front of your mouth. Blow and suck gently a few times to make the eardrum move to and fro (vibrate). Now make a hole (a perforation) in the tissue paper and blow and suck again. The paper should not move so much this time. This shows that the hole weakens the vibration of the eardrum.

EXPLORING THE EAR

Hermann Helmholtz (1821–1894), a German scientist, studied the ear and attempted to explain how sounds are heard. He was the first to realise that the cochlea was important in converting sound waves into electrical messages that travel along nerves to the brain.

HEARING AIDS

People who are not deaf but cannot hear very well often wear a hearing aid. A hearing aid contains a microphone, an amplifier and a loudspeaker (see pages 28–29). The microphone picks up sounds reaching the ear, the amplifier makes the sounds louder and the loudspeaker plays the amplified sounds into the wearer's ear.

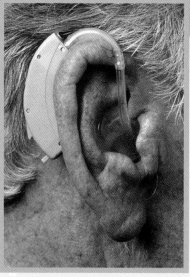

Modern hearing aids are so small that you hardly notice when someone is wearing one.

THE SPEED OF SOUND

We get most of our information about the world from sound and light. Both sound and light travel as waves, but in other ways they are very different. One difference, the difference in their speeds, has been used to work out the speed of sound.

HOW LIGHT AND SOUND ARE DIFFERENT

We saw on page 7 that when Boyle made a vacuum inside a glass jar, and then rung a bell inside the jar, it made no sound. However, the bell was still visible inside the jar. This shows that light can travel through a vacuum, but sound cannot.

When lightning flashes at a distance, you see the flash straight away, then several seconds later hear a roll of thunder. The two things actually happen at the same time, but light travels much faster than sound, so we see the lightning first.

SOUND IN LIQUIDS AND SOLIDS

Air is a gas, and sound travels through all gases. It travels through liquids and solids too. However, the particles in liquids are much closer to each other than the particles in gases. This allows sound to travel faster and further than it does in a gas. In solids, the particles are even closer together and conduct sound waves even faster than in liquids. However, because the particles in a solid cannot move so easily as those in a liquid, the vibrations do not travel as far (see page 7).

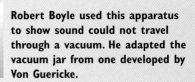

Robert Boyle used this apparatus to show sound could not travel through a vacuum. He adapted the vacuum jar from one developed by Von Guericke.

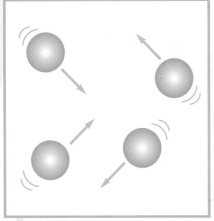

■ particles in a gas

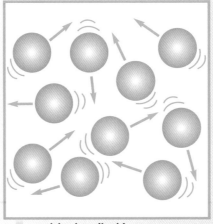

■ particles in a liquid

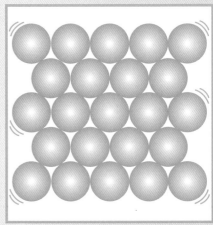

■ particles in a solid

SOUND SPEEDS

The speed of sound in air changes with temperature. For example, at 0°C sound moves at 330 metres per second and at 20°C it travels at 343 metres per second. The reason for this is that warmer air particles have more energy and can conduct sound faster.

The speed of sound does not change as much with temperature in liquids and solids. Sound travels at 1500 metres per second in water and at 6000 metres per second in steel.

MEASURING THE SPEED OF SOUND

Ask a friend to stand 150 metres away and clap together two small blocks of wood. You will see the movement instantly, but the sound takes longer. When you see the pieces of wood clapped together, start a stopwatch. When you hear the sound, stop the stopwatch. What do you calculate the speed of sound to be?

HEARTBEATS AND CANNONS

Marin Mersenne (1588–1648), a French monk, asked a friend to stand some distance away and fire a gun. He saw smoke rise from the gun and then heard the sound. As there were no accurate watches in his day he counted his heartbeats between seeing and hearing the gun fire. From this he worked out that sound travels at 450 metres per second.

William Derham (1657–1735), an English scientist, stood at the top of a church tower and watched a cannon being fired 19 kilometres away. He had a more accurate clock than Mersenne and recorded the time between seeing the cannon flash and hearing its roar. He found the speed of sound to be 343 metres per second, which is remarkably accurate.

SOUND WAVES

You cannot see sound waves, but scientists can convert the invisible waves into waves that you can see. They do this by using a microphone (see pages 28–29) to pick up the sounds and turn them into electrical signals. They then feed the signals into an oscilloscope. This is an instrument with a screen similar to the one in your television. The oscilloscope displays the sound waves on the screen.

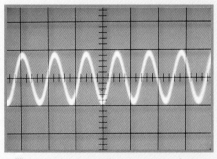

A sound wave shown on an oscilloscope screen.

The main features of a wave are its wavelength and its amplitude. They are related to how the particles within the wave are moving.

The amplitude of a wave shows how much the particles in the wave are vibrating. In a wave with a high amplitude, the particles vibrate a lot, but in a wave with a low amplitude they vibrate much less.

The wavelength of a wave tells you how quickly the particles in it are vibrating. A small wavelength means fast vibrations, while in sound waves with a long wavelength, the particles vibrate more slowly.

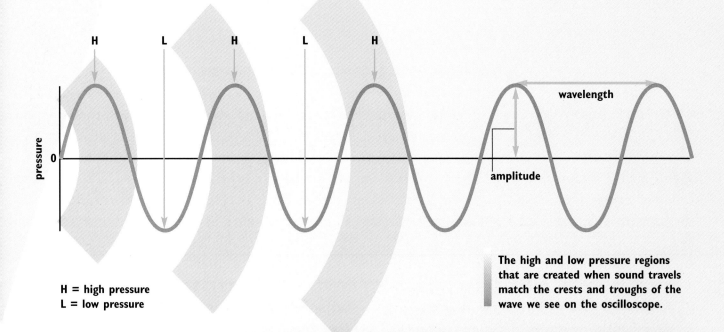

H = high pressure
L = low pressure

The high and low pressure regions that are created when sound travels match the crests and troughs of the wave we see on the oscilloscope.

THE SHAKING MIRROR

Dayton Miller (1866–1941), an American scientist, invented a device called a photodeik, which helped him to visualise sound. A spot of light was shone onto a mirror and reflected onto a screen. When sound waves struck the mirror they made it vibrate and the light spot moved up and down.

SOUND AND ENERGY

Energy has many different forms and can change from one form to another. Sound waves are form of energy. A loud sound has a lot of energy, while a quiet sound has much less energy.

SHAKE THAT ROPE

It is easy to understand that waves have energy if you make waves in a length of rope. Tie one end of a rope to a door handle and shake the other end gently. Do you use a lot of energy? Do the waves have large or small amplitudes? Now put more energy into shaking the rope. Do the waves get smaller or bigger?

Try shaking the end of the rope slowly, and look at the length of the waves you produce. Now speed up, and shake the rope quickly. How does the length of the waves change? You should see that when you speed up your shaking, the wavelengths get shorter.

REFLECTIONS OF SOUND

When a sound wave strikes a surface, some of its energy is absorbed. But some of the sound is reflected back into the air. Hard, smooth surfaces are the best sound reflectors. If sounds are made in a room with hard smooth surfaces, the sounds are reflected many times and make a slight echo called reverberation.

To hear a clear echo rather than reverberation, the sound reflection needs to reach your ear at least a tenth of a second after the original sound. Otherwise, your ear cannot separate the echo from the original.

TEST THE THEORY

Sound travels at about 340 metres per second, so in a tenth of a second it travels 34 metres. The sound travels away from you and then back again, so how far would you need to be from a wall or other reflecting surface before you could hear an echo?

Find a quiet place where there is a high wall and test whether you can actually hear an echo when you are this distance away from the wall.

THE PITCH OF SOUNDS

Sing the word 'high…' as high as you can. Now sing 'low…' as deep as possible. You are singing sounds of different pitches. The 'high' sound is high-pitched and the 'low' is low-pitched.

The pitch of a sound is related to the length of its sound waves. Long-wavelength sounds are low in pitch, while high-wavelength sounds are high-pitched.

FREQUENCY AND WAVELENGTH

When an object vibrates, it does not just produce one sound wave, but many waves every second. If the sound waves have a short wavelength there are lots of waves per second. If the waves have a long wavelength there are fewer waves per second.

Scientists call the rate at which sound waves are produced the frequency of a sound. So a sound with a long wavelength has a low frequency, while one with a short wavelength has a high frequency. Low-pitched sounds have a low frequency, and high-pitched sounds have a high frequency.

The unit for measuring frequency is the hertz [Hz]. In a sound wave of 100 Hz, for instance, there are 100 waves per second. You can hear sounds ranging in frequency from about 20 Hz to 20,000 Hz.

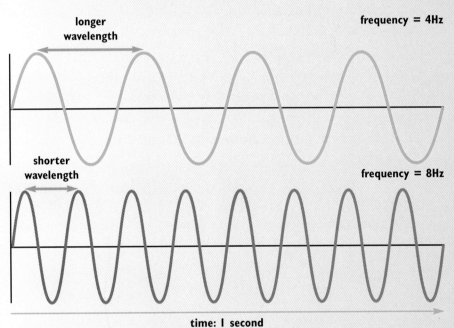

These two sound waves have different frequencies. The lower wave has twice the frequency of the upper wave. Both waves have frequencies below the range of the human ear.

ELASTIC GUITAR

Find three elastic bands the same length and thickness, and three erasers. Close this book, and stretch the bands around it. Put an eraser under each elastic band as below. Now press a finger on one of the bands where it passes over the eraser, and pluck. Try plucking the other two bands in the same way. You should get three different notes. How does moving the erasers affect the notes you get?

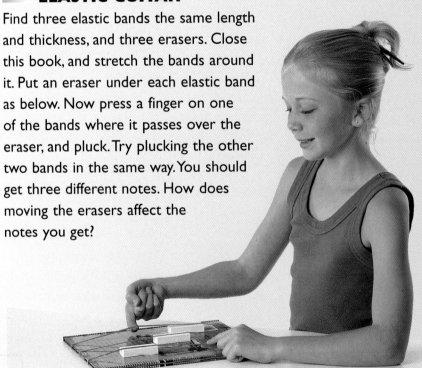

RESONATING

When a length of elastic band is plucked, the whole length vibrates and it produces a sound of a certain frequency. Most objects have a frequency at which they will vibrate. If they receive sound waves at that frequency, they themselves will vibrate and produce a sound. This is called resonance.

If a brittle object resonates too much, it can shake itself to pieces. This can happen when a singer hits a note with the same high frequency as a wine glass. The wine glass shatters.

This painting on an ancient Greek vase shows a musician playing a lyre. This was the most common stringed instrument in ancient Greece.

On 7 November 1940, the Tacoma Narrows Suspension Bridge in the USA had been open only a few months. High winds that day started the roadway resonating, and within a short time the bridge had shaken itself to pieces.

Pythagoras (582–487 BC), a Greek philosopher, studied the sounds made by stringed musical instruments. He discovered that if the length of a vibrating string was shortened, the pitch of the note was raised. He also discovered that if one string was half the length of another one it produced a sound with a pitch that was eight notes (an octave) higher on a musical scale.

MAKE A RESONATOR

Take two identical empty glass bottles. Hold one close to your ear, and blow across the top of the other one. You are making a sound in the one close to your mouth but you will also hear a similar sound produced by the other bottle as it resonates.

CHANGING PITCH

Have you noticed that the pitch of the siren on an ambulance changes as it approaches you, then rushes by? The change is due to something called the Doppler effect. When the ambulance is stationary, the siren sends a steady stream of sound waves to your ear. But if it is moving towards you, the sound waves are pushed closer together and their frequency and pitch increase. When the ambulance passes you and moves away, the sound waves are stretched out. They reach your ears less frequently and the pitch drops.

We hear the Doppler effect in action when an ambulance or fire engine drives past.

LISTEN TO THE DOPPLER EFFECT

Attach a whistle to one end of a flexible plastic pipe with sticky tape. Blow down the other end of the pipe so that the whistle sounds. Still blowing, swing the the pipe so that the whistle end of it goes round in a circle, rising and falling in front of you. Does the pitch of the whistle's note change? When does it rise and when does it fall?

THE MUSICAL TRAIN

Christian Doppler (1803–1853), an Austrian scientist, noticed how the pitch of sounds changed when the source passed by him quickly. He worked out a relationship between the peed and the way the pitch changed. He tested his idea in the following way. He put trumpeters in a train, made them play a certain note and had the train move along at different speeds. Standing by the track were a group of musicians who could recognise the pitches of notes accurately. The musicians by the track identified the changes in pitch as the train went by. Their observations matched Doppler's calculations.

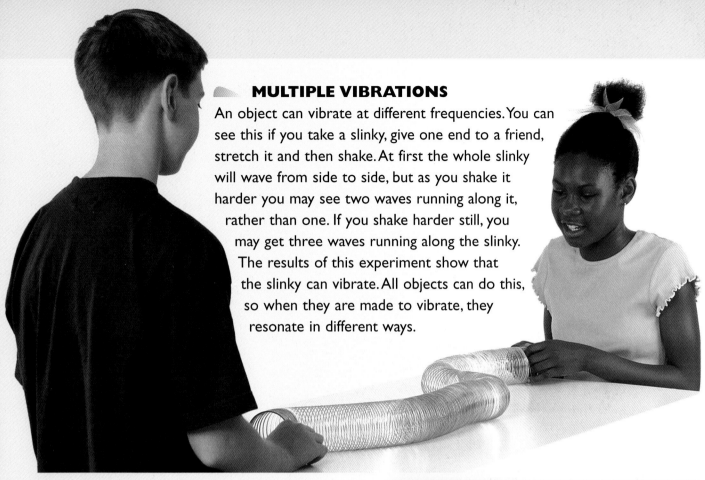

MULTIPLE VIBRATIONS

An object can vibrate at different frequencies. You can see this if you take a slinky, give one end to a friend, stretch it and then shake. At first the whole slinky will wave from side to side, but as you shake it harder you may see two waves running along it, rather than one. If you shake harder still, you may get three waves running along the slinky. The results of this experiment show that the slinky can vibrate. All objects can do this, so when they are made to vibrate, they resonate in different ways.

MUSICAL VIBRATIONS

A clarinet and a violin sound different, even if they are playing the same tune. This is because an instrument does not produce one pure sound wave. When the instrument plays a note, it vibrates with a range of frequencies. One frequency, called the fundamental, is stronger than the others and makes the note we hear. But there are also other weaker vibrations with different frequencies, which are called the harmonics or overtones. Different instruments have different overtones, which is why they sound different.

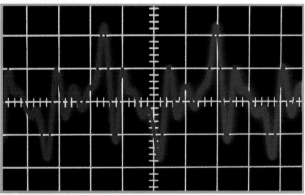

Because the sound is made up of several different frequencies, the wave produced by a musical instrument is more complicated than a simple up and down wave.

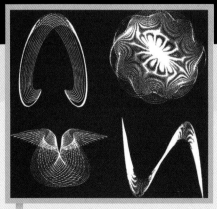

Some Chladni figures.

PATTERNS IN THE SAND

Ernst Chladni (1756–1827), a German scientist, covered thin plates with sand and set them vibrating. He found that the sand was shaken off parts of the plate and settled on others, forming patterns on the plate (now called Chladni figures). The patterns differed, depending on the frequency of the vibration. They helped Chladni understand how materials vibrated when they were set in motion.

THE LOUDNESS OF SOUNDS

Read this paragraph aloud. Begin with a tiny whisper and gradually make your voice louder and louder until you are shouting. When you have finished reading, you should realise that making a loud sound uses more energy than making a quiet one! When you raise your voice, you give more energy to the air particles around you, which gives them bigger vibrations.

LOUDNESS AND DISTANCE

It may have sounded loud when you shouted out words from this book. But if you had been outside, people a few hundred metres away would not have noticed. This is because as the particles in the air vibrate and produce a sound wave, they use up energy. So the sound waves become smaller as they move away from you, and the sound waves become quieter and quieter until they can no longer be heard.

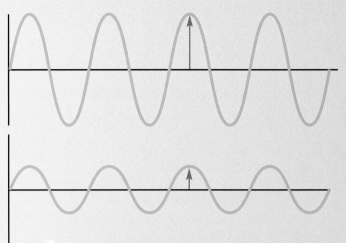

These two sound waves are the same pitch (same wavelength), but the top one is louder (the amplitude is bigger).

HOW FAR DOES THE SOUND TRAVEL?

Set up a radio in a large space like a hall. Turn it on but keep the volume low. Walk slowly away from the radio until you can no longer hear it. Now measure the distance you have walked. Go back to the radio and turn up the volume. Predict how far you will have to walk this time before you can no longer hear it. Test your prediction – how accurate was it?

MEASURING LOUDNESS

The unit for measuring the loudness of a sound is the bel, named after Alexander Graham Bell (see panel). Sounds are usually measured in decibels (dB), which are tenths of a bel.

The decibel scale is not like the scale on a ruler, where 20 centimetres is twice the value of 10 centimetres. On the decibel scale, 20 decibels is not twice, but ten times louder than 10 decibels, and 30 decibels is 10 times louder than 20 decibels (100 times louder than 10 decibels). A scale that measures in this way is called a logarithmic scale.

THE DECIBEL SCALE

	LOUDNESS
160dB	ears permanently damaged
140dB	military jet taking off
130dB	sounds become painful
110dB	road drill
100dB	front rows of pop concert
90dB	heavy traffic on busy road
80dB	vacuum cleaner
70dB	normal street traffic
60dB	busy department store
50dB	people talking
30dB	whispering
20dB	rustling of falling leaves
10dB	limit of human hearing

HOW LOUD IS IT?

Use the decibel scale to assess the loudness of the sounds around you now. Make assessments at other times of day. At what time of day do you think the noise level is loudest?

KEEPING THE BOOM AWAY

Some jet aircraft can fly faster than sound. When they do so, they produce a massive build-up of air pressure called a shock wave. This makes a huge bang called a sonic boom, which contains so much energy that it can vibrate windows until they break. Aircraft flying faster than sound have to fly high. This way, the energy in the shock wave is reduced by the time the sound reaches the ground, and it does not cause damage.

Supersonic (faster than sound) planes like these are highly streamlined. This he to cut down on the size of the sh wave when they fly faster than

THE FIRST SOUND ON A TELEPHONE

Alexander Graham Bell (1847–1922) was a Scottish inventor who was also a teacher of deaf children. He believed that sound waves could be converted into electrical currents and that the electrical currents could be converted into sound waves. He developed a device that did just that. It was the first telephone.

When Bell was about to test his device, he accidentally spilt acid on his clothes and called out. His assistant, in another room, heard Bell's call through the telephone and rushed in to help.

MAKING MUSIC

Try shouting out a musical scale: 'do, re, mi…'. Now try singing the notes. Which sounds pleasanter? Singing is easier on the ears than shouting. The reason for this is that musical sounds are orderly vibrations called regular vibrations. A shout is a noise, and like all noises it is made from less orderly vibrations called irregular vibrations.

MAKING THE SOUNDS

Most musical instruments make sounds in one of three ways: by plucking strings (stringed instruments), by blowing to create vibrations (wind instruments), or by hitting something to produce a note (percussion).

STRINGED INSTRUMENTS

In a stringed instrument, the note a string produces depends on the length of the string and on how much it is stretched. Players play different notes by pressing their fingers on the strings, to change the length that is vibrating. But when a guitarist tunes his instrument, he uses pegs on the ends of the strings to tighten or slacken each string until it plays the right note.

In an acoustic stringed instrument such as a guitar or a violin, the strings are attached to a hollow wooden body. This is called a resonator. When a string vibrates, the walls of the resonator and the air inside it also vibrate. These extra vibrations make the sound louder.

Sound resonates inside the hollow body of an acoustic guitar. An electric guitar has a solid body. It does not need a resonator, because it is amplified electrically (see page 28-29). This guitar uses both acoustic and electric amplification.

TEST A RESONATOR

Stretch an elastic band around a piece of wood and push an eraser under the band. Pluck the elastic band and listen to the sound. Now put the wood over the top of a bowl and pluck again. You should hear a louder sound due to the bowl acting as a resonator.

WIND INSTRUMENTS

When you blow a wind instrument such as a recorder or a flute, the air inside it vibrates. It makes a wave that does not leave the instrument, called a standing wave. The particles vibrating in the standing wave make the sides of the instrument vibrate, too. This produces sound waves in the air around the instrument.

The length of the standing wave inside the instrument is controlled by the fingers opening and closing holes in the instrument. When all the holes are closed, the standing wave has a long wavelength and low frequency – we hear a low note. When all the holes are uncovered, the standing wave has a shorter wavelength and higher frequency – we hear a high note.

The bottom part of a drum is a resonator. If you hit drums like these when they are on a table, they make a dull sound. This is because the resonators do not work properly when the holes at the bottom are blocked.

PERCUSSION INSTRUMENTS

Percussion instruments are played by being hit or shaken. Many are used to provide a rhythm and to add to loud sections in a piece of music. Many percussion instruments do not play exact notes: they make noises rather than musical notes. However, instruments such as xylophones and tubular bells do play different notes – they are known as tuned percussion.

Two main types of percussion instrument are drums and cymbals. A drum has a tight skin that vibrates when it is hit. The sound of the drum can be changed by changing the tightness of the skin. Cymbals are made of metal and are designed to give a ringing sound. They may be tapped to keep the rhythm or crashed together to make a loud noise.

ANIMALS AND SOUND

If you rest your fingers on your throat and start to hum, you should feel a vibration. It occurs in your larynx or voice box. Other animals that have a larynx are frogs and toads, a few reptiles and most mammals. Birds have a voice box called a syrinx to help them sing. Insects such as crickets make sounds by rubbing their wings or other body parts against each other.

INSIDE THE LARYNX

The larynx is made from hoops of a tough material called cartilage, held together by muscles. Inside are two flaps called the vocal cords. When you breathe in, the vocal cords are pulled aside to let air into your lungs. If you want to speak or sing, the vocal cords move towards the centre of the larynx and vibrate as you breathe out.

WHY EVERYONE'S VOICE IS DIFFERENT?

The vibrations of the vocal cords set off sound waves in the air inside your throat. The air in your mouth and nose also vibrates. The size and shape of these air spaces is different in each person, and this produces the unique sound that is your voice.

YOUR MOUTH

You can see how changing the shape and size of an air space in your head alters the sound you make, by altering the shape of your mouth. Look in a mirror and say 'A, E, I, O, U'. See how the shape of your mouth changes as you form each letter.

SPEAKING OR SINGING

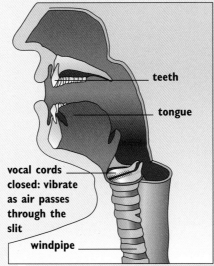

teeth

tongue

vocal cords closed: vibrate as air passes through the slit

windpipe

BREATHING

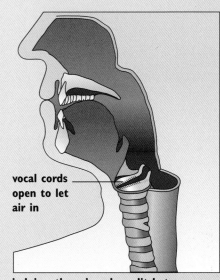

vocal cords open to let air in

When the vocal cords are across your windpipe, there is only a slit between them. Air passing through the slit makes the vocal cords vibrate.

FROG SOUNDS

When a frog is about to make a sound it fills up two pouches, one each side of its mouth, with air. The pouches act as resonators, and make the sounds the frog makes louder. Frogs can make a range of sounds – honks, whistles, chuckles, and even quacks!

In places such as rainforests, many different kinds of frog live together. Each kind makes calls in a certain range of frequencies, and its ears are particularly sensitive to sounds of these frequencies. This helps the frogs to recognise the calls of their own kind and ignore those of other frogs.

BIRD SONG

Instead of a larynx, birds have a syrinx. This is at the bottom of the windpipe, where it divides into two tubes (one going to each lung). The syrinx has a membrane that acts like a vocal cord at the opening of each tube. A bird can make sounds using either membrane, or it can use both together and sing a duet with itself!

INSECT SOUNDS

Some insects use the hard outer parts of their bodies to make sounds. Grasshoppers make sounds by rubbing their back legs against their wings. Crickets have a file on one wing and a scraper on another. When they rub them together they make a chirping sound.

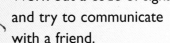

TALKING INSECT

Try making some insect sounds of your own. Use a comb as a scraper and a pen as a file. Make noises by scraping the pen on the comb. Work out a code of signals, and try to communicate with a friend.

COMMUNICATING CHIMPS

Jane Goodall (born 1934), a British scientist, studied groups of chimpanzees in Africa. She lived closely with them and observed their daily lives. She discovered that they used about twenty different sounds as a simple language to communicate with each other.

SOUNDS WE CANNOT HEAR

We saw on page 14 that you can hear sounds ranging in frequency from 20 Hz to 20,000 Hz. As people get older, they cannot hear high-pitched sounds so well, and they may not be able to hear sounds above 12,000 Hz. Other animals can hear sounds of much higher or lower frequencies. Sounds above or below human hearing are called ultrasounds and infrasounds.

SEEING WITH ULTRASOUND

Sonar stands for SOund NAvigation Ranging. It is used on ships to 'see' underwater. Sonar equipment sends out beams of high-frequency ultrasound, which reflect back off objects in the water. A detector in the sonar equipment picks up these underwater echoes.

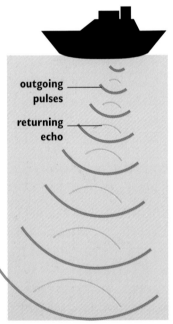

outgoing pulses

returning echo

Sonar can be used in various ways. Ships use sonar to detect the depth of the sea and so avoid running aground. Submarines use sonar to spot obstacles while they are underwater. Geologists on research ships use sonar to look for underwater valleys and mountains. The crews of fishing boats use sonar to find shoals of fish.

ECHOLOCATION

Bats and dolphins have been using their own kind of sonar, called echolocation, for millions of years. They produce streams of high-pitched ultrasounds, and their ears pick up the echoes that bounce back off objects around them. Bats use echolocation to catch insects, while dolphins use it to find shoals of fish.

VIBRATING CRYSTALS

Pierre Curie (1859–1906), a French chemist, found that when crystals of quartz were pressed, they generated a small amount of electricity. Later, other scientists reversed the process and fed small amounts of electricity through quartz crystals. When they did this, the crystals vibrated and produced ultrasounds. Paul Langevin (1872–1946), a French scientist, developed a device for sending ultrasounds and a device for detecting them. These devices were the basis for the sonar equipment used today.

INFRASOUND

Think of a rumble of thunder, or the throbbing bass sounds of a pop record. Infrasounds are sounds even lower than this. Elephants and whales use infrasound to communicate. Deep powerful sounds made by elephants can travel many kilometres across a grassy plain. They help members of a group keep in touch at a distance. In water, sound travels faster and further than in air (see page 7) so whales can communicate using infrasound when they are over a thousand kilometres apart.

CALCULATING WAVELENGTHS

You can calculate the wavelength of a sound if you know its frequency and the speed of sound. For example, the lowest sounds that humans can hear have a frequency of 20 hertz. If sound travels at 340 metres per second in air (see page 11), the wavelength of these sound waves is 340/20 = 17 metres.

The highest frequency you can hear is 20,000 Hz. What is the wavelength of these sound waves? Hint – you will need to measure in millimetres (thousandths of a metre). Draw a few of these waves on a piece of paper.

An elephant can produce sound waves with a frequency of 8 Hz. How long are sound waves of this frequency? Mark one out on the ground.

SCANNING WITH ULTRASOUND

When a woman is pregnant with a new baby, doctors often use ultrasound to check that the fetus is growing healthily inside the womb. Beams of ultrasound are directed into the womb, and reflect from the surface of the fetus. The ultrasound echoes, coming back from the fetus, are collected by a receiver. A computer uses the information from the receiver to build up a picture of the fetus on a screen.

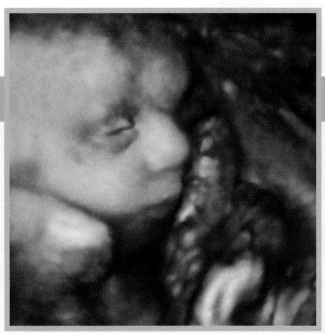

Here you can see an ultrasound image of a four month old fetus.

NOISE POLLUTION

You often hear people say they would like some peace and quiet. You may think that they are being fussy and that there is nothing wrong with noise. However, this is not true. Many people find it difficult to think properly and relax in noisy surroundings. This in turn can affect their health and make them feel stressed. Loud noises can affect health in another way. They can damage our ears and hearing – sometimes permanently. Noise can be controlled by modifying the way it is transmitted and reflected.

REDUCING TRANSMISSION

The transmission of sound means the movement of sound from its source to your ears. If the source of sound is a radio, you can simply turn down the volume. Many machines make loud sounds that cannot be turned down. However, the sound from a machine can often be reduced using sound insulation material. This material absorbs energy in the sound waves and reduces their amplitude (see pages 8-9) to make the sounds quieter.

Some people work with loud machines that cannot be insulated. The engine of a chainsaw, for example, gets so hot that any insulation material around it would catch fire. To protect their hearing around such machines, people wear ear defenders (see picture). These are pads containing sound insulation material that fit over the ears.

TESTING MATERIALS

Make a collection of different materials, such as wool, cotton, plastic sheeting and bubble wrap. Set a radio at a certain volume and wrap it in one material. Move away from the radio and measure the distance at which you can no longer hear it. Repeat the test with the other materials. Which one is the best sound insulator?

ABSORBING SOUND

Surfaces that are soft and rough absorb more sound than hard, smooth surfaces. You may hear this difference when you move house, or if you take all the furniture out of a room to decorate it. Without sound-absorbing objects such as beds, sofas and curtains, the sounds in a room are louder and slightly echoey. When a room is furnished, the softer surfaces absorb sound and make the room quieter.

BOUNCING SOUND WAVES

You can simulate sound waves hitting hard or soft surfaces in the following way. Ask a friend to hold up a wooden board and gently throw a tennis ball at it. Notice how far the ball bounces off the board. Now change the board for a cushion and throw the ball again. What happens when the cushion absorbs most of the ball's energy?

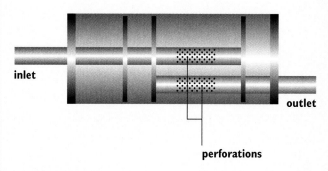

inlet

outlet

perforations

A cutaway of a car silencer. The perforations in the tubes allow thousands of tiny sound pulses to escape from the pipe and bounce around inside the silencer.

Car and truck engines are noisy, because they explode fuel to make them work. The loudness of the sound is reduced by attaching a silencer to the exhaust pipe. As the sound waves move through the silencer, they reflect off the walls of the pipes and chambers inside. The sound waves end up 'out of step' with each other: the high pressure section of one wave matches up with the low pressure part of another. When this happens, the sounds cancel each other out.

OUT OF THE WINDOW

Wallace Sabine (1868–1919), an American scientist, noticed that sound could be lost from a room by opening a window. He used this observation as a measurement of how materials absorbed sound. For example, using his scale, a material in a room may absorb sound as if the room had one, two, three or more open windows. He also studied the way rooms echoed and found ways of reducing the echo in large buildings such as concert halls, so that music could be heard clearly. His discoveries are used by architects when they design large buildings where performances take place.

SOUND TECHNOLOGY

Scientific discoveries about sound go hand in hand with advances in technology – the invention of useful devices such as hearing aids, telephones and stereos. Most sound technology, from CD players to radio communications from the Earth into space, rely on two inventions – the microphone and the loudspeaker.

Microphones convert sound waves into electric signals (small changing currents). Loudspeakers do the opposite – they convert electrical sound signals back into sound waves. Both these inventions are possible because of the way magnets and electricity behave.

Microphones and other sound technologies enable us to communicate with each other across great distances. Here a pilot is able to speak to support crews on the ground and at sea.

MICROPHONES

There are many different kinds of microphone, from small, simple ones used in telephone handsets to high-quality microphones used in recording studios.

One of the most widely used types is called a moving-coil microphone. This has a sound-collecting device called a diaphragm – a thin sheet of material that vibrates when sound waves strike it. The diaphragm is attached to a coil of wire surrounded by a magnet.

As the diaphragm vibrates, the coil moves to and fro inside the magnet. The movement of the wire in a magnetic field produces pulses of electricity in the wire. These pulses are an electric 'copy' of the sound waves causing the diaphragm to vibrate. This electric copy is called a sound signal.

SOUND SIGNALS

If the microphone is being used by a pop singer at a concert, the sound signals will pass to an amplifier and then on to a loudspeaker, where they will come out much louder. If the microphone is being used by a presenter at a radio or television studio, the pulses of electrical energy will travel along wires and through the air as radio waves until they reach your TV or radio. Here the signals will be changed back into sounds in a loudspeaker.

magnet

coil attached to microphone

movement of coil in magnet makes electric signal in wire

LOUDSPEAKERS

A loudspeaker has a cone made of stiff paper or similar material, attached to a coil of wire. The wire is surrounded by a magnet. When the electrical sound signals travel through the coil of wire, the magnet pushes and pulls on the coil, making it vibrate. This causes the paper cone to vibrate and produce sound waves.

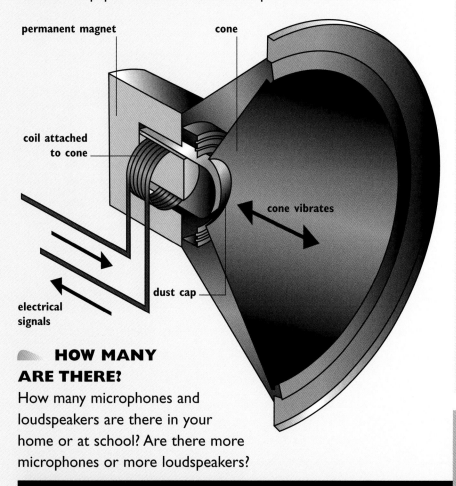

permanent magnet

cone

coil attached to cone

cone vibrates

electrical signals

dust cap

HOW MANY ARE THERE?

How many microphones and loudspeakers are there in your home or at school? Are there more microphones or more loudspeakers?

THE FIRST RECORDING

Thomas Edison (1847–1931), an American inventor, made the first sound recording in 1877. He recorded the sound on an invention called the phonograph. He spoke the words of the rhyme 'Mary had a little lamb' into a receiver (a kind of microphone), and it made a needle cut a groove in a cylinder of wax. Later, the needle was made to run through the groove while attached to a loudspeaker. The vibrations of the needle vibrated the loudspeaker and played back the sound of Edison's voice.

VOICE RECOGNITION

Everyone's voice is unique: people's voices all sound different, and they talk in different ways. Computer programs have been developed so that a person's voice can be identified from the electrical signal they create by talking into a microphone. This is then used as a kind of 'voice signature'. Only the person with the right voice signature can access private information on the computer. There are also programs that allow a computer to 'take dictation'. You speak to the computer instead of typing in words on a keyboard, and the computer writes what you say.

Thomas Edison, in later life, using the technology he pioneered

29

TIMELINE

Pythagoras (about 582–487 BC), a Greek philosopher, studied the sounds made by stringed musical instruments and discovered a relationship between the length of the string and the pitch of the note it made when it was plucked.

Aristotle (384–322 BC), a Greek scientist, believed that sounds travelled through the air in a similar way to waves travelling across water.

Marin Mersenne (1588–1648), a French monk, measured the speed of sound, using his heartbeat to time how long it took to travel a set distance.

Otto Von Guericke (1602–1686), a German scientist, created a vacuum and showed that sound could not travel through it.

Robert Boyle (1627–1691), a British scientist, proved that sound couldn't travel through a vacuum.

William Derham (1657–1735), an English scientist, made the first really accurate measurement of the speed of sound.

Ernst Chladni (1756–1827), a German scientist, used sand and vibrating thin plates to understand how materials vibrated when they were set in motion.

Christian Doppler (1803–1853), an Austrian scientist, studied how the pitch of a sound changes when its source approaches and then moves away.

Hermann Helmholtz (1821–1894), a German scientist, studied the ear and identified the place where sound waves are changed into nerve messages to the brain.

Alexander Graham Bell (1847–1922), a Scottish-born American inventor, made the first microphone and developed the telephone.

Thomas Edison (1847–1931), an American inventor, made the first sound recording.

Pierre Curie (1859–1906), a French chemist, found that when crystals of quartz were pressed, they generated a small amount of electricity. This led to the development of devices that produce ultrasound.

Dayton Miller (1866–1941), an American scientist, invented a device called a photodeik, which helped him to visualise sound.

Wallace Sabine (1868–1919), an American scientist, studied how echoes could be removed from large rooms. His discoveries are used by architects today.

Paul Langevin (1872–1946), a French scientist, developed devices that are the basis of modern sonar equipment.

Jane Goodall (born 1934), a British scientist, discovered that groups of chimpanzees use about twenty different sounds as a simple language to communicate with each other.

GLOSSARY

acoustic – a musical instrument that can be played without needing to be amplified electrically.

amplitude – the maximum height of a sound wave or other vibration.

cartilage – a tough, flexible substance used to strengthen and support some parts of the body.

conduct – to allow something such as a vibration to pass.

decibel – a unit for measuring the loudness of sound.

energy – the ability of matter or waves to perform work such as movement.

fetus – an unborn baby developing in its mother's womb.

frequency – the rate at which a sound wave or other vibration repeats itself.

infrasound – sound waves that are too low-pitched to be heard by the human ear.

insulation – when material does not allow sound to pass through it.

membrane – a very thin skin.

magnetic field – the area around a magnet where its magnetism acts.

nerves – thin fibres that carry messages around the body in the form of electrical currents.

octave – a group of eight notes.

oscilloscope – an instrument that converts and displays sound waves visually on to a screen.

percussion – instruments that produce a musical sound when they are struck or shaken.

pitch – how high or low a sound is. Pitch is related to the frequency of a sound wave.

pressure – a pushing force over an area of a surface.

receiver – an electrical device that converts sound energy into electrical energy.

quartz – a kind of crystal, often milky white, made from a rocky substance.

radio waves – invisible waves that can travel very fast through the air. The sounds and pictures on our radios and televisions reach us as radio waves.

resonate – to vibrate strongly in response to sound waves.

resonator – a device that resonates strongly in response to sound waves and makes the sounds louder.

reverberation – a slight echo.

standing waves – waves that remain stationary in the air or on the string where the vibration takes place.

ultrasound – sound waves that are too high-pitched to be heard by the human ear.

vacuum – completely empty space, containing no air or any other material.

vibrations – rapid to and fro or up and down movements.

wavelength – the distance between one wave and the next.

INDEX